# MAKE AND CREATE
# CLAY MODELING
## AND
# PAPIER MÂCHÉ

Written by Nat Lambert

Models by Gary Kings

Published by Top That! Publishing plc
Tide Mill Way, Woodbridge, Suffolk, IP12 1AP, UK
www.topthatpublishing.com
Copyright © 2013 Top That! Publishing plc

# Papier Mâché
# Getting Started

It's amazing what you can make with papier mâché! For centuries people have made anything from puppets and toys to furniture! Papier mâché is so popular because it's cheap and easy to use.

The term papier mâché actually comes from France. French women used to buy paper waste and process it by chewing it. Don't worry though, you won't have to do that to make the models on the following pages!

Before you start making the models you'll need to prepare your work space and gather all your equipment together. Make sure you choose a place where you can leave your models to dry. Always cover your work space with newspaper and make sure that your clothes are covered as well.

From a cat to a tortoise, a monster to a dog, you'll have lots of fun completing the projects ahead, but remember—be patient! To create the projects on the following pages you will need glue powder, poster paints, a paintbrush and round balloons—you can get hold of the materials from specialist art or craft stores.

Other items that you will need can easily be found around the house. Strips of newspaper, stiff card, double-sided sticky tape or glue, a black marker pen, string, a cardboard tube, a drinking straw, masking tape, aluminum foil and a needle are all needed to make the models. Always ask an adult to help you when using a needle or any other sharp object!

## OTHER PROJECTS

Remember, once you have completed the projects on the following pages, you can have great fun creating your own papier mâché characters!

**Warning!** ⚠️
Always keep uninflated balloons and other papier mâché materials out of the reach of small children.

# Basic Techniques

### BALLOONS
Before you begin making your model, blow up a balloon. This forms the basic shape of the model and it's a good surface to stick your paper strips on. Keep the balloon steady with some sticky putty stuck to your work surface.

### PAPER STRIPS
The most important material for modeling is the paper. Cut lots of strips of newspaper into 1 in. squares. These are used to cover your balloon at the start. Make sure you prepare plenty of strips before you begin because your hands might get a bit sticky.

### GLUE PASTE
To make the paste, add a packet of glue powder to four pints of water. Mix well and store in a re-sealable container. If you cannot get hold of glue powder, use wallpaper paste or mix one part of flour to two parts of water.

## SIMPLE SHAPES

When it comes to putting the strips on the balloon, there is a technique you will need to master. If the paper is soaked for too long in the paste, it can be quite difficult to work with. Try dipping your fingers into the paste and smoothing it over the paper until it is slightly soaked. Once the paper is soft it can be easily laid over the balloon. Cover small areas first to check that it sticks on okay —it wouldn't be much fun if your paper slipped off halfway through what you are doing!

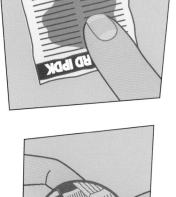

## FEATURES

To make special features, such as eyebrows and noses, you'll need to make up a pulp. A simple pulp can be made by dipping your strips of paper into the paste until it is soaked. Mold the pulp into the shape you want and place onto your model. To keep the pulp in place, lay a slightly soaked strip of paper over the top and then smooth over with your fingers, using a small amount of paste. Leave your models to dry by hanging them on string from a curtain rail or, if it's a sunny day, leave them to dry outside for about 2–3 hours.

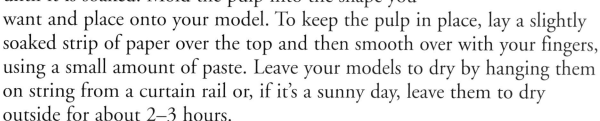

# ALLY the CAT

1. Blow a balloon up to about 4 3/4 in. in length and cover it with 3–4 layers of papier mâché. Then tie a piece of string around the knotted end of the balloon and hang it up to dry thoroughly.

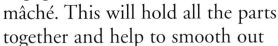

2. To make the feet, copy the template, below, onto a stiff piece of cardboard, making it about 3 in. long. Cut this out carefully. Draw and cut out the template three more times to give four identical foot shapes.

X4

3 in.

3. Using the templates from step 2 as a base, make the cat's feet. Use a ball of scrunched-up papier mâché for each toe. Bulk up the rest of the foot gradually until you get the shape you want.

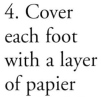

4. Cover each foot with a layer of papier mâché. This will hold all the parts together and help to smooth out each shape. Place them somewhere warm to dry.

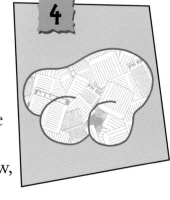

5. To make the head, copy the template, below, onto a stiff piece of cardboard, making it about 3 1/2 in. square. Cut this out carefully and use this as a base to build up your cat's head shape. Next, create cheeks and a mouth area from balls of scrunched-up papier mâché.

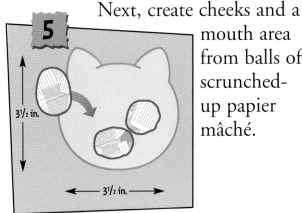

3½ in.

3½ in.

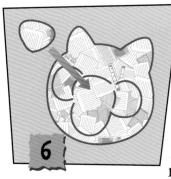

6. Bulk up the front and back of the head with more papier mâché, making sure you also build up the back of the cat's ears. Mold a small triangular nose and add this to the head. Then cover the whole head with a layer of papier mâché to hold everything in place. Leave to dry thoroughly.

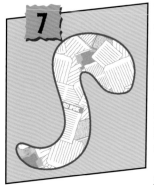

7. Make the tail by scrunching and molding a large amount of papier mâché into an uneven "S" shape, making sure the large end is rounded. Cover it with a layer of papier mâché and leave to dry.

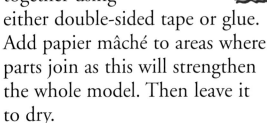

8. When all the individual parts are dry, stick them together using either double-sided tape or glue. Add papier mâché to areas where parts join as this will strengthen the whole model. Then leave it to dry.

9. Finish your model by painting it. Use a black marker pen to add details such as eyes, eyebrows, whiskers, claws, a nose and a mouth. Purr-fect!

## TOP TIP!
**Why not glue some whiskers onto your alley cat using some string!**

# DEREK the DOG

1. Blow a balloon up to about 4 3/4 in. in length. Wrap a length of masking tape around its middle as tight as you can to force it into the shape shown. Cover this with 3–4 layers of papier mâché. Then tie a piece of string around the knotted end of the balloon and hang it up to dry.

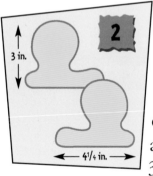

2. To make the hind legs, copy the shape, left, onto a stiff piece of card, making it about 4 1/4 in. x 3 in. Cut it out, then draw around it and cut a second shape out.

3. Using the templates from step 2 as a base, make the legs with scrunched-up papier mâché. Make sure that the top half of each leg is flat on the inside, as this will help when you join it to the body.

Cover each leg with a layer of papier mâché and leave to dry completely.

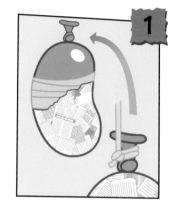

4. To make the forelegs, copy the diagram, below, onto a stiff piece of card, making it about

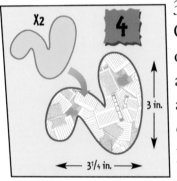

3 1/4 in. x 3 in. Carefully cut it out. Draw around this again and then cut it out so you have two identical foreleg shapes. Bulk these out gradually with papier mâché.

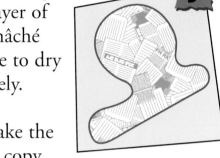

5. Blow up another balloon to about 3 1/2 in. in length. Cover this with 3–4 layers of papier mâché and hang it up to dry. This will eventually form the dog's head.

6. Make the tail by scrunching and molding some papier mâché into an uneven sausage shape, making sure the narrow end is rounded. Bend this slightly and then cover it with a layer of papier mâché. Now leave it to dry.

7. Copy the shape, right, onto some stiff card and cut it out. Draw around this again and then cut it out so you have two identical

shapes. Stick these onto the head. Mold and add a small triangular nose shape and a long, oval tongue shape. Add a layer of papier mâché to hold everything in place.

8. When all the individual parts are dry, stick them together, using either double-sided tape or glue. Add extra papier mâché to areas where the parts join to strengthen the whole model.

Add a tongue and two ears to the head and leave it to dry.

9. Finish your model by painting it. Use a black marker pen to add details such as the eyes, spots and a black line on the tongue.

# SHELLY the TORTOISE

1. Blow a balloon up to about 4 3/4 in. in length. Cover this with 3–4 layers of papier mâché. 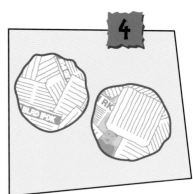 Tie a piece of string around the knotted end of the balloon and hang it up to dry.

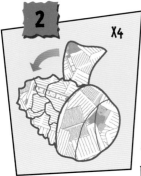 2. Make the tortoise's four legs from scrunched-up papier mâché covered by a smooth layer of papier mâché. Round the thinner ends of each leg and then leave them to dry.

3. Scrunch some more papier mâché into a chunky sausage shape before gently molding it into the head shape. Add a mouth with a little more papier mâché. Smooth and strengthen this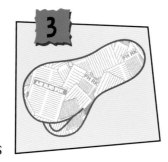

shape by adding a final layer of papier mâché all over. Leave it to dry.

4. Mold two small balls of papier mâché for the tortoise's eyes. Place these to one side to dry.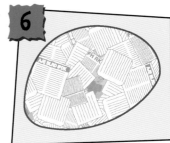

5. To make Shelly's tail, mold some papier mâché into a cone shape. Smooth it over by covering it with a layer of papier mâché and then leave it to dry.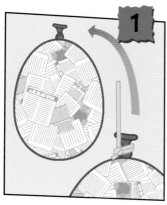

6. When the papier mâché, applied in step 1, has dried, pop the balloon and remove it. Cut the balloon-shaped papier mâché in half to form a basic shell shape.

7. Add a long, thin, scrunched-up sausage of papier mâché to the edge

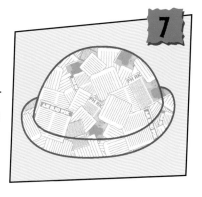

of the dome. Smooth this off and hold it firmly in place by covering it with a layer of papier mâché. Put this to one side to dry. This completes the shell.

8. When all the parts have dried, stick them together, using either double-sided tape or glue. Cover all the areas where parts join with a layer of papier mâché as this will strengthen the whole model.

9. Glue the two balls of papier mâché from step 4 to the top of the tortoise's head. Paint your model, adding two eyes and details with a black marker pen.

**TOP TIP!**
**Experiment with colors! Why not make a friend for Shelly and make them bright and colorful with paints!**

# IRIS the MONSTER

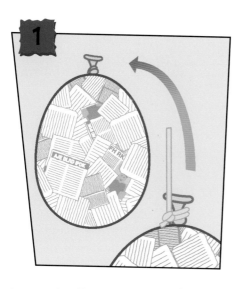

3. Using the template from step 2 as a base, mould the feet components. Use a ball of scrunched-up papier mâché for each toe. Bulk up the rest of the foot until you get the shape you want. Place it to one side to dry.

1. Blow a balloon up to about 4 3/4 in. in length. Cover this with 3–4 layers of papier mâché. Tie a piece of string around the knotted end of the balloon and hang it up to dry.

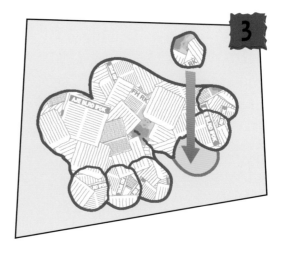

2. To make the feet, copy the template, below, onto a stiff piece of card, making it about 6 in. x 4 3/4 in. Cut this out carefully.

4. When the papier mâché covering the balloon has dried, carefully mold a bottom lip and chin shape onto it.

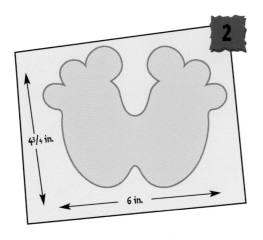

12

5. Put six bumps of papier mâché down the length of the monster's back. Cover them with a layer of papier mâché as this will hold them in place.

6. Mold three medium-sized balls of papier mâché for the monster's eyes. Place these to one side to dry.

7. When all the papier mâché covering the balloon is dry, pop the balloon and remove it. Stick all the parts together using either double-sided tape or glue. Cover all the areas where parts join with a layer of papier mâché and leave to dry. Finish your model by painting it. Use a black marker pen to outline details.

**TOP TIP!**
**Make sure you have plenty of newspaper strips—you don't want to be tearing more if you have sticky hands!**

# *Clay Modeling*
# Getting Started

## Modeling Mechanics

The following pages teach you everything you need to know to create a selection of cool clay model sculptures! You'll really be inspired to create a variety of quirky designs of your own.

Before you begin, make sure your hands are clean and you have a flat, clean surface to work on. To complete the projects, you will need self-hardening clay, a handy modeling tool to help with the fiddly bits and a practice pad for you to sketch your own cartoon sculpture creations before you start modeling. All of these materials can be easily purchased from specialist art and craft stores.

The cartoon sculptures would make ideal gifts, or you could start your own collection of crazy models. Don't delay—get sculpting today!

## *Top Tip*

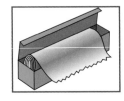

Make the most of your materials with this handy hint. Use aluminum foil to pad out the insides of large areas of clay. This will make your supplies last longer, and will also stop models with large heads from becoming top heavy and falling over.

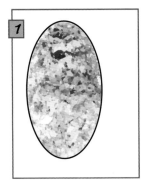

### *Step 1*
Take a piece of aluminum foil and screw it up into a ball. This will form the center of your object.

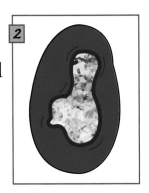

### *Step 2*
Now mold the clay around the foil ball, completely concealing it. Make sure the surface of clay is smooth.

# Tools of the Trade

Your most valuable modeling tools are your hands, so keep your nails short and use the tips of your fingers to achieve the best results. You can buy more specialist clay tools from craft stores which will help you craft shapes that are difficult to mold by hand. Disposable plastic cutlery also make useful tools.

Goggle eyes lend a really professional touch to your models. Don't worry if you can't find them though—tiny balls of white clay with a black marker pen to add eyes works just as well! You can buy goggle eyes fairly cheaply in most craft stores.

# Combining Colors

Combine different colors of clay to create different shades! Purchasing these four colors will enable you to make an array of shades.

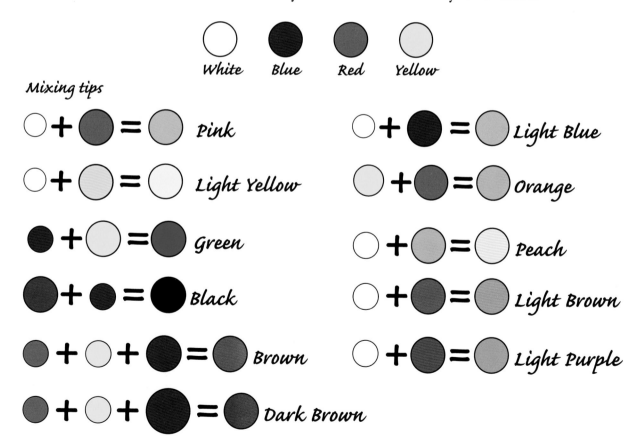

To make colors lighter add white and to make colors darker add black.

# Hands, Feet and Paws

Create convincing body parts for your models by adapting these simple steps.

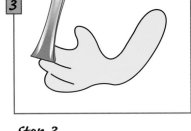

## Hands

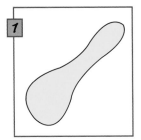

### Step 1

Begin by rolling a ball of clay into an uneven sausage shape. Flatten and round the large end until you end up with a spoon shape.

### Step 2

With a modeling tool, make four cuts into the spoon shape to create a hand. Cartoon characters usually have only three fingers!

### Step 3

Round off the edges of each finger and the thumb with a modeling tool. Finally, bend the fingers and thumb into the pose that you want and bend the middle of the arm to form an elbow.

## Feet

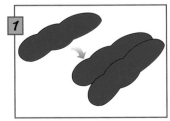

### Step 1

Start by rolling three balls of clay; large, medium and small. Now, roll each into an uneven sausage shape and round all the ends.

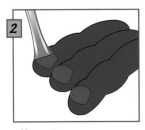

### Step 2

Place them side-by-side. With a modeling tool, make all the indents shown at the large end of each sausage.

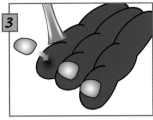

### Step 3

Roll three tiny balls of clay. Flatten these and add one to each toe to form toenails. Make the markings shown with a modeling tool.

## Paws

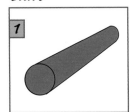

### Step 1

Begin by rolling a ball of clay into an uneven sausage shape. Round both ends.

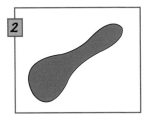

### Step 2

Flatten and round one end to form a shoulder. Shape the larger end as shown.

### Step 3

Make two indents with a modeling tool and round off. Bend the paw and arm into a pose that suits your model.

# Manic Monster

*This three-eyed monster is so scary!*
*Make him and scare all your friends!*

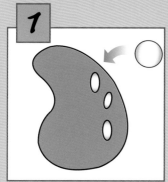

1. Mix a ball of light purple clay and mold into the shape shown, to form Manic's body. Flatten several tiny balls of white clay into various sized spots and add these to his back.

2. Roll six orange clay balls into sausage shapes, making one end bigger than the other. Round each end off and place in two lines of three. Make the markings shown with a modeling tool to create Manic's two feet.

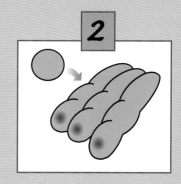

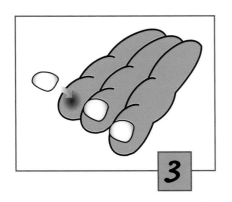

3. Roll six tiny white clay balls in three sizes. Flatten these as shown and add one to the tip of each toe to create toenails.

4. Roll two evenly sized balls of orange clay and make each one into an uneven sausage shape. Flatten the large end of each sausage and shape it into a claw, as shown. Flatten and round the other end of each arm and attach to either side of the body section made in step one.

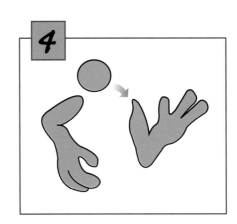

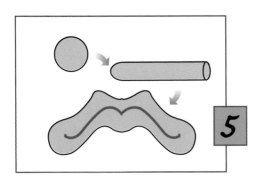

5. Mix a medium-sized ball of pink clay and break in half. Roll both halves into long, even sausage shapes and then join them together. Shape it into the mouth shape, as shown.

6. Roll two small pairs of white clay balls, making one pair slightly smaller than the other. Mold each of these into the tooth shape shown. Use a modeling tool to make two indents in the middle and one at each end of the mouth. Place the teeth into these indents, putting the smaller ones in the middle of the mouth.

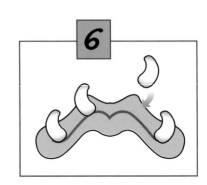

7. Add the finished mouth to the bottom of the monster's body, as shown.

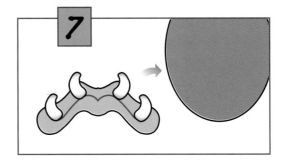

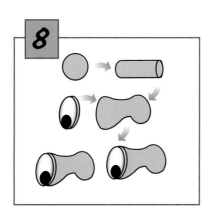

8. Roll three identically-sized balls of pink clay into cone shapes. Bend them and place them side-by-side to create Manic's eye stalks, as shown. Place a goggle eye on the end of each stalk, or try balls of white clay, using a marker pen to add pupils.

9. Once you have completed the three eye stalks, add them to the top of the monster's body, as shown.

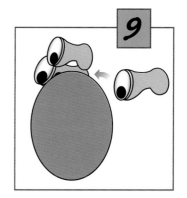

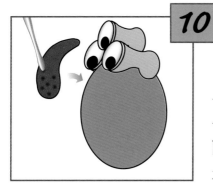

10. Roll some dark purple clay into a small, uneven sausage shape. Attach it to the body to make his nose. Texture the tip of his nose by using the point of a modeling tool to make a series of dots.

11. Roll a small and large ball of dark purple clay. Flatten and shape the small ball into a triangle, and roll the large ball into an uneven sausage. Attach the triangle to the thin end of the sausage, then flatten and round the other end of the sausage. Bend this into the shape shown to create Manic's tail.

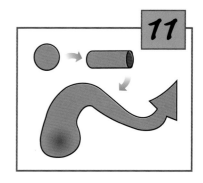

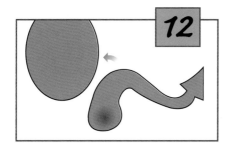

12. To complete your Manic Monster, simply attach the tail to the base of the body, smoothing over the join to create a seamless effect. Get ready to scare your friends!

# Vroom! Vroom!

*This sporty little motor is sure to get your engine running!*

1. Mix a large ball of dark brown clay and break this into four balls of equal size. Roll each of these into sausage shapes of equal thickness and length, and bend each sausage into a circle, joining the ends together. Shape four equal-sized balls of red clay into dome shapes and fix one behind each of the circles, as shown.

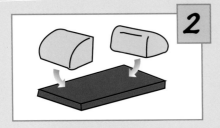

2. Flatten a large ball of blue clay into a rectangular shape. Roll two large light blue balls of clay. Mold the two large balls into the shapes shown, then add them to the rectangular shape.

3. Roll four large, equally-sized balls of blue clay into uneven sausage shapes—they must be of equal length and thickness. Flatten each slightly and round the ends and sides, as shown.

4. Place the four wheels from step 1 at each corner of the body made in step 2. Bend the shapes made in step 3 over the top of each wheel to form the wheel arches. Lift the car's body off the ground and support it with something while you correctly position the wheels.

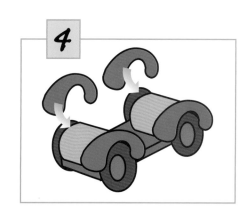

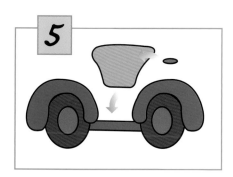

5. Roll two small light blue balls of clay then mold them into the shapes shown. Place one on either side of the car, between the front and back wheel arches to make the doors. Place a small sausage of red clay on each door to make handles.

6. Roll two red clay sausages that are the width of the car. Place one at the front and one at the rear to form the car's bumpers. Roll four small red clay sausages and place two on each bumper, as shown.

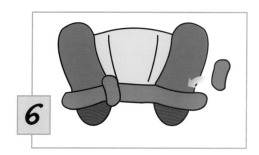

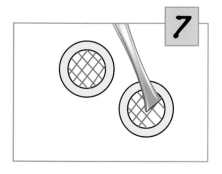

7. Roll two small balls of yellow clay, two yellow balls half the size of those and two white balls, even smaller still. Flatten them all into disk shapes, and add the white ones to the large yellow ones. Add markings, as shown, to complete the headlights.

8. Place one headlight on top of each front wheel arch. Position the two small yellow disks on each rear wheel arch, at the same height as the front headlights.

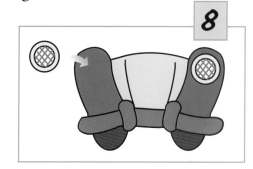

9. Roll two yellow balls of clay. Flatten one into an oval shape and make the markings shown. Roll the other into a thin sausage shape, place it round the edge of the oval and place on the bumper, as shown, to form the car's license plate.

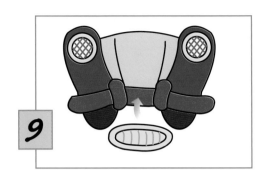

10. Roll a small ball of blue clay into an uneven sausage shape and round off the ends to make them smoother. Place them on the hood, as shown.

11. Roll a ball of white clay and mold it into the flattened shape shown. Add a flattened sausage of blue clay to this and position on the hood, as shown, to complete the windshield.

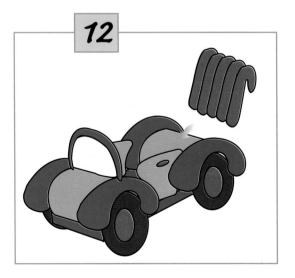

12. Roll five red balls of clay into sausage shapes of an equal length. Place them side-by-side, then bend one end of this line of tubes over. Position them in the car, as shown, to complete your car.

# Fairy-tale Castle

*This multi-turreted palace looks tricky but it's really very simple.*

1. Roll a medium ball of light purple clay, and another slightly smaller one. Split the medium-sized one into four balls of equal size. Roll each of these balls into a squat cone shape, making sure they are all the same height and thickness.

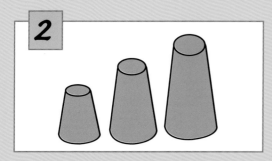

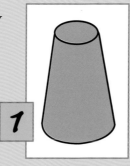

2. Take the other ball of light purple clay and split it into three balls; a large, medium and small one. Roll each of these into a squat cone shape. Each one should be a different size to the four made in step 1.

3. Roll a large ball of red clay and split it into two balls, one slightly larger than the other.

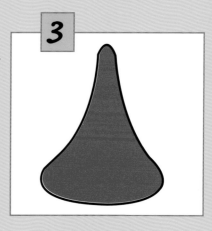

Take the larger ball and split it into four balls of equal size. Roll each of these into the cone shape shown. Make sure they are all the same height and thickness.

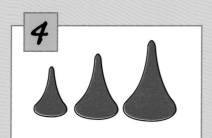

4. Split the other ball of red clay into three balls; large, medium and small. Roll each into a cone shape, just as you did in step 3. Make sure they are all different sizes.

5. Roll a ball of purple clay and split it into seven smaller balls of equal size. Mold each of these into sausage shapes and flatten each one slightly. Wrap one around the thin end of each cone shape, as shown. Join the ends together and make the markings shown with a modeling tool.

6. Use a modeling tool to add four windows to each of the four equally-sized towers. Then add three windows to the tallest tower, two windows to the middle one and one window to the smallest one. Add the correct-sized red turret to each tower.

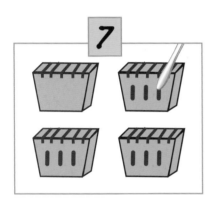

7. Roll five equally-sized balls out of light purple clay, and flatten four of them into wedge shapes. Flatten the remaining one into a square. Use a modeling tool to add the markings shown to three of the wedge shapes. Leave the fourth bare.

8. Roll a small ball of purple clay and flatten it into a door shape, as shown. Add it to the wedge shape with no window markings on it. Score in three vertical lines with a modeling tool. Now, roll four equal-sized pink balls of clay. Add one ball to the top of each equally-sized turret.

9. Use the remaining three wedge shapes, made in step 7, to join the towers, started in step 1, so that they form a square. Arrange the three remaining towers onto the flattened light purple square made in step 7. Place this inside the four walls to add stability to the overall structure, and to complete your fairy-tale castle.